JAIDA RENEE AND KENDRA ASHANTI

We Are Already Here

Poetry from Two Lives told in Five Parts

First published by Jaida Renee & Kendra Triblet 2019

This is a work of creative nonfiction. Some parts have been fictionalized in varying degrees, for various purposes.

First edition

ISBN: 978-0-578-55061-9

Cover art by Sam Smith
Cover art by Carla Lopez

This book was professionally typeset on Reedsy.
Find out more at reedsy.com

Contents

IV   Edumacation: On a Campus and Playground near You

V   Here

I

Check-in: Queens, NYC

I walked like my borough was my namesake
And I spoke like a Nas album –
Saturday's
Even those grey and rainy
Sound to me
Like everything.

3

When Kashif tickled my coochie and touched my flat titties in the cafeteria

I knew that's what boyfriends did to girlfriends.
   Didn't mean I liked it though.
   I told my mommy and daddy -
   Kashif dumped me after my daddy pressed him
   In the hallway outside the classroom.
   It was my first dramatic breakup, and I cried.
   I felt bad that I got him trouble -
   Apologized for my own violation.
   A trend of feeling sorry for men not having access to my body.
   A pattern of feeling ashamed of my virginity.
   What did I know then? Except everything that I didn't.
   Years later I tried to remember Kashif's full name -
   So I could look him up online
   Not to apologize for getting him in trouble -
   That's just what boyfriends do, right? -
   But so that I can tell him that I had thought that we were meant to be
together
   Because "J" and "K" were right next to each other
   Whenever we said our ABC's.

-J

how to be a Lady

May 27th 1995

Begins the story of me, Kendra Ashanti
  On a rainy Saturday I arrived
  Not yet knowing
  I was already amazing
  Already a sensation
  Already being groomed
  And taught
  And trained
  And compartmentalized to sit like a lady
  And Wear pink
  And Go talk to that boy over there
  But don't get too close to the boys
  And most of all, Be a lady
  I cross my legs, pull down my skirt
  Look at, but don't touch the boys
  Put pillows in my shirt, I got boobies
  Smear Mommy's lipstick on, I'm a lady
  I strut with a purpose
  I stand with a presence
  I hug the wall to make room
  In the tub, I wash my kitty cat
  I don't let nobody see

Mommy and Daddy said not to
I'm pretty, I'm private
I'm a real lady
A girl two years older than me
She got real boobies
Like two little cherries
My friend shows me hers, like two little lemons
I can't show them mine
I'm one little cereal box, flat all over
Daddy says be a Lady
But it doesn't matter
Cuz the boys say i'm Ugly
Since i got no boobies, no booty
i pretend my kitty cat is invisible
Without my boobies, she might as well be.
Without my boobies,
i can't be a lady
Without a boyfriend,
i must be ugly.
When someone asks why i'm so quiet
i say i'm a kitty cat
They think i mean to say i'm crazy
But i mean to say that just like the kitty between my legs
i'm invisible
i am nothing special.
i am unimportant.
i am not amazing.
i am unsensational.

-K

Claudine's Father

Being black and being a child feels like

Do as I say but not as I do
  Me and your mother just talkin
  Don't fear nobody but God
  Get out that fridge
  Don't end up like me
  Finish your food
  Don't bring home no babies
  You betta be in that bed
  Don't let that teacher call my house
  I betta not hear you say, "I don't know"
  Don't make me go up to that school
  You betta hit them back
  Don't get in this store and act a fool
  "You got McDonald's money?"
  Don't make me embarrass you
  Shut up fore I give you something to cry about
  Don't let nobody walk all over you
  Sit down somewhere
  Don't worry about them kids teasing you
  Fix your face
  What you afraid for?
  I ain't raise you to take no

For an answer
Why?
Because I said so

-J

Them Three Little Girls

We were always them three little girls

Me, my best friend, my other best friend
   Long, gangly limbs
   Yeah, we were those three
   They'd fight, I'd break it up
   We'd all fight and make up
   Compare our legs, laugh about them dirty little boys
   Yeah, we were them three little girls
   Then my best friend left, other one changed schools
   And we all got new best friends
   We became strangers
   Having distant phone conversations
   Until slowly, slowly, slowly
   We became nothing more
   Than virtual friends - MySpace top eight -
   Slowly turned from them girls
   To that girl,
   That girl,
   And that girl.

-K

Good Hair

First perm, age 6

Mommy, it burns!
  But it's just a thought
  I suffer, I cringe
  To get my silky crown
  I want Good Hair
  The comb gliding through
  Not breaking a single tooth
  My hair in two long pigtails
  Longer than my sister's
  I got Good Hair
  I need a perm every four weeks
  Dominicans flying past me
  Burning my ears from the heat
  Of the flat iron
  The blow dryer
  I have to endure it
  I need Good Hair
  And over the years
  My hair, thin and lifeless
  Creamy crack is all I know
  But sometimes my curls will show
  When I take out my braids

Admire the waves
That I've melted away
Admire the crown
That I've shunned with dismay
Trapped between torture and
The foreign, monstrous fro
Begrudgingly, to the salon chair I go
With no desire to wear my real crown
To endure the burns, the heat,
At age 15, so familiar to me
I hate Good Hair

-K

black girl blonde hair

for every black girl who ever existed in South Jamaica Queens

only cuz
    my eyelashes flap in the wind like wings on my face,
    my oversized topknot is too silky to blend in with my naps,
    my PINK brand backpack matches the Vicki's Secret cheetah print bra
    I'm showing off through my white Hollister shirt
    that I begged my mama for last week.
    my uggs are the same color as my J's and the same color of my contacts
    that I bought from the Colli block the same day me and Rise got our
belly buttons pierced
    by the Jamaican dude with the black lips and fingertips.
    my North Face is the flyest in my school
    even though I don't know how my grandma could afford it
    with her social security check on hold and her disability not coming
in.
    my boyfriend is the cutest nigga in 11th grade
    and he know it too, so I stay having to fight bitches
    for trying to press what they know is mine.
    me and my bad bitches fuck it up every weekend
    we love double-chained rappers from behind double-chained bed-
room doors
    cuz my parents don't trust me to go out with them no more
    since she caught me and Rise at Wayne's house with our shirts off.

I still see Wayne at school though, and he rides the 111 with me after school
    sometimes we sneak to the Ave. to make out in the multiplex.
    only cuz I get down like that.

-J

L.I.G.

Legend has it that if you ride the Q5 too far into
Laurelton you'll hear so many Jamaicans you'll think
you're in Kingston

But you're in Queens
   We are royalty.
   I learned that my borough was my namesake when a boy told me only
"good" girls came from Queens.
   I had reveled in variations of "good" up until that point –
   Had not been blessed with good hair –
   But I had good grades and came from good stock
   My family was not rich or poor in money, but if you asked, I would
say "we good."
   I would say "What's good," when I travelled to other parts of the city
   My crown tipped ever so slightly upon my micro braids –
   Niggas was tight how they be on the first day –
   Because even though I never intended to
   I walked like my borough was my namesake
   And I spoke like a Nas album
   Because, indeed, Life was Good
   And no matter how hard I tried I couldn't deny my lineage –
   You can shoot the nose off the pharaoh but that don't erode his
greatness –
   I couldn't deny that I came from legend

And I was always content with just being good
But I was afraid to think that I could be better.

-J

Rainy Saturday

Saturday's, grey

The color of soot
  Sound to me like
  Cereal and cartoons
  Barbies and Ballet school
  The freedom to choose
  The imagination to create
  The energy to cultivate a unique day
  Saturday's to me sound like
  Movies with daddy
  Trips to the park with mom
  Scraped knees walking home
  At the second darkest hour
  Ashy hands looking like
  I've been playing in flour
  Birthday parties
  Gardening and junk food
  Saturday's
  Even those grey and rainy
  Sound to me
  Like everything

-K

II

Interlude: A Tale of Two Cities

If a Black woman falls while standing
on her own two feet,
does her body make a sound?
–J.

Deforestation - the death

Fuck the 4 train and Spanish men,

Because I am a strong and dark they think I don't need a seat
   They don't see me as delicate
   Or tired
   Or deserving
   I watch them get up for pretty Spanish women
   I pretend not to see, not to care, to hurt
   Because I can hold my own.
   I don't want no special treatment.
   So when I enter strong and careful to not make eye contact –
   Because that is the New York way –
   They think I don't need a seat
   They don't see the way I shift my weight
   From being on my feet all day teaching their children
   They don't see me as delicate
   Or tired
   Or deserving
   Because
   They don't see me.

-J

Leaving

Has always been hard for those with black skin

The fear the fear the fear it drives us
    Consumes us
    Self-sabotage
    I cannot change cannot grow cannot break free
    Cycles
    Generational trauma
    More than a buzzword
    My life my reality - I cant grow
    Cant be brown and grown and unloved
    Pick a struggle

-J

This One's called the Affect and the Effect (Thanks, Sommer Browning)

This poem was written in 2012, but it's still relevant today. I left the blanks for you to insert your modern reference as you please.

And this one's called Chicago Is Actually Mobile, Alabama With A Willis Tower

and this one's called Gentrification Matriculation

and this one's called I Just Learned What Redlining Is and Why The White Kids Don't

Ride It Past 35th

and this one's called The Usurping of Everything, Even the Ghettos

and this one's called _____'s Plan to Remind Us That 9/11 Happened

and this one's called All McDonald's Commercials Are Targeted To the Black Community

and this one's called McDonald's is Ran By _____

and this one's called That Would Be Funny If It Was

and this one's called But I Still Won't Stop Eating It

and this one's called Word, We All Die Anyway

and this one's called True That!

and this one's called I Like Harold's Better, Though

-J

Homeboy Homeostasis - the life

I got on the 2 train at Jackson ave

Three young men of certain hues were sitting
  Taking up space
  No one else could sit there.
  They weren't talking
  Each was listening to music,
  But they bopped their heads in pattern –
  A conversation.
  Obeying all commands –
  Be quiet –
  As boys in the Bronx are often told.
  Sit down –
  As boys in the Bronx are often told.
  They were Defiant –
  As boys in the Bronx often are.
  They reminded me of my students –
  Beautiful.
  I felt the frustration from tired straphangers
  Nine to fivers who just wanted to slump in a seat
  Sleep
  Perhaps
  But had to stand and watch these young men
  In their rhythm

In the silence
In their loudness
In their everywhereness all over those seats.
And although I was one of the weary nine to fivers,
I felt an immense pride
And I watched them, thinking,
"Take up space in the world, young man.
Take up as much space as you can."

-J

III

Interlude: A Black Girl goes to Europe

And with all those foreign smiles
I fell in love with exploration
With my courage
With myself.
–K.

ig'nant.

Every time I hear surprise

Dripping from the voice of a man
  Marveling at how smart I am
  I can't help but wonder if the shock
  Is due to my gender
  My race
  Or my nationality
  But all three are a hindrance
  And place me at the end of the intelligence spectrum
  That no pretentious asshole would ever be caught dead on
  As a woman, I have the privilege
  Of letting men be smart
  And trusting them to make decisions
  And allowing their voices to be louder
  As a black person, education is not my priority
  I am too consumed with my struggle
  I don't deserve
  I can't afford
  To waste institutional space
  Or fulfill an affirmative action quota
  As an American, I'm permitted and expected
  To be blissfully unaware
  To know that I am a product of a world superpower

To know that the world is watching us
And praying for us when we're attacked
And protecting our wealth
And laughing behind our backs - sometimes to our faces
So between the three l just can't pinpoint which identity
Makes me the presupposed idiot.

-K

Aus von der Dunkelheit

(Author's note: I did not use anything to edit this poem, because I wanted it to accurately capture the extent of my German writing comprehension, mistakes and all.)

Ganz allein in der Hauptstadt
   Fühle ich stolz auf mich?
   Ich bin nur 22 Jahre alt
   Und schon hab' ich mein Heimat verlassen
   Um neue Umgebungen zu erkunden
   Um neue Leute kennenzulernen
   Um ein bisschen unbequem zu sein
   Oder fühle ich mehr als ein bisschen unbequem?
   Wie kann ich zu meiner Familie sagen
   Dass ich ein Fehler gemacht habe?
   Dass ich mich einsam fühle?
   Dass die Deutschkurse waren nicht genug?
   Manchmal muss ich eine Witze dreimal hören
   Manchmal sag ich "ja" wann die Kellnerin fragt
   "Was fur ein Saft willst du?"
   Immer hasse ich mein Akzent
   Ausländerin steht auf mein Gesicht
   Soll ich zurück nach Hause gehen?
   Meine Freundin sagen dass ich verrückt bin
   Mein Papa schreibt mir jeden Tag

Und Mama weint manchmal, weiss ich schon
Vielleicht bin ich verrückt
Aber meine Entscheidung
War die erste Entscheidung dass ich gemacht habe
Ohne die Bestimmung meiner Eltern
Angst kontrolliert mich nicht
Fur Einsamkeit habe ich kein Angst
Und jetzt kann ich das madchen Kendra
zu die Frau Kendra vergleichen
Immer noch habe ich Angst
Aber jetzt verstehe ich
dass das Leben das ich fur mich gemacht habe
Die Leute die ich jetzt Freunden nennen kann
Die Erfahrungen, gut und schlecht die ich hätte
Sind grosser und wichtiger
Als Angst
Jetzt verstehe ich was Freiheit heißt
(Der U-Bahn kommt)

-K

DRKSKNGRL

I move through this world glistening and glittering

Catching the eyes of all
   Through hands that wish to touch ethereal skin
   Run their hands through nappy bountiful hair
   To be black anywhere in this world is a beautiful thing
   For what I once perceived as hate
   I now translate into admiration
   Because there is nothing more mesmerizing
   Than to see a Queen
   Strutting, gliding, prancing
   Through Primark
   Waiting to buy 4 euro sneakers

-K

For the First Time

It scared the shit out of me.

The first time I went to a country
  With more consonants than people,
  More syllables than sidewalks.
  The cold, hard building looming over me
  Sun retracting into the clouds
  I was afraid of who I had become
  Wondering why I had to be so damn brave
  Now ain't that ironic.
  Wandering the streets
  Staring up at the colorful cathedrals
  All the colors in the world
  Could not pull me away from that feeling
  Of being foreign
  Of being isolated
  Of being alone
  My wandering feet took me far
  As I was willing to go
  To walk away from the reality of my discomfort
  My feet took me to a tiny cafe
  Where I got lost in a book
  In poetry of love
  I pushed the world out until

The magic of the poetry moved me to tears
And I wanted to love, too
I wanted to love that little country
That city that's fraction of mine
And its people, excited to teach me
Their language and their city's gems
I had people to show me the beauty of nature
And food so good, you'd cry
And the clubs where you could lose yourself
In all the best ways
I was not alone
I had more company than just books
I had a country with more passion than hate
With more open arms than borders
And it was there in that tiny country
With all those syllables
And with all those foreign smiles
That I fell in love with exploration
With my courage
With myself.

-K

IV

Edumacation: On a Campus and Playground near You

Some of y'all only got the chance to be one thing in life so far
– you had interests turned majors turned fields of studies
turned careers,
But I got to be mad shit in one lifetime.

Ntozake's Recycling Bin

For colored girls

Who have considered a Master's degree
  When a bachelor's was not enough
  For those who could not even make
  The commitment to college
  Because high school was plagued
  With naysayers and systemic
  Trauma
  Obama-era recessions in a post-Bush economy
  For those whom for college was a commodity
  Not of their pockets
  But of their integrity and peace of mind
  For those who could not afford to go to an HBCU
  For those who signed their lives away to go
  For the parents who co-signed away their empty nest years
  For those who pore over the statements each month
  Perhaps with cheap wine
  Perhaps with tears
  Always with anxiety
  Always with a lingering gratefulness for their experiences
  Languid kicks in proverbial asses for being so fucking optomistic
  For those who believed
  That college equaled a good job

One that your parents didn't have the opportunity for
Except your good job never came
Or came too late
Maybe you didn't network enough
Maybe your liberal arts degree lost its luster
But this is for ya'll
For us
Because our education just wasn't enough
Too bad we didn't have the balls to just be all we could be.

-J

Known

When one of my students asked me, "Why do white kids get into better colleges?"

I told her, "It's not because they're smarter. It's the belief that they are better."
    She didn't know how to compete.
    I wanted to hug her and whisper, "My dear black girl, it is not enough
    To *be* smart and inspiring
    You must *believe* that you are more than."
    Instead I said, "It's belief that got Trump elected. Many
    White people believed and it happened."
    I asked her how many times
    She had heard people in our community
    Say their vote did not count.
    Who did not believe.
    Who did not yes we can the fuck out of an election.
    She rolled her eyes and replied, "Well, actually Hilary won the popular vote."
    And just like that
    Majority ruled all over my damn argument.
    "Yeah, but," I replied,
    "Everyone still believed Trump did."

-J

Ode to Smart Black Girls

Take pride in your intellect

Don't shy away from it
  Like they shy away from
  Using the word "black"
  Instead of "African American"
  Don't turn your back on it like they turn their heads
  When someone brings up urban youth
  Don't cover it up the way they cover up institutionalized racism
  With the importance of individualism
  And hard work
  Wear it, like the crown you never reappropriated
  Own it, like you own your golden brown skin
  Breathe it, like the air of America
  Clogged with the debris of
  False Hope
  And in the wind, you will hear
  The tiniest whisper of a voice
  Singing
  We Shall Overcome
  Someday.

-K

I am not your Anomaly.

Someone asked me

"How did YOU even get in this school?"
   I rode right in on the affirmative action train of course
   I know that's what you're inclined to believe
   Whenever you look down your nose at me
   My mama thinks this school's got me stressed
   What she doesn't know is
   Her daughter's depressed
   A hot mess
   I don't belong with private tutoring Ryan
   And 2400 SAT Joe
   And the work is tough
   So I don't try as hard
   Because I know no matter what,
   I'll only get half as far
   The years pass me by
   And long after I have shed the insecurity
   Of my intellect
   Like a winter coat
   I realize I cheated myself
   All because I thought
   Private tutoring Ryan was on a whole 'nother boat
   Same school, same subjects,

Only difference is hue
And as much as a little pigment can do
I encourage my brown
And black girls
To read, read, read
Write, learn, absorb
Think, grow, project
Expect nothing to be handed to you
Go chase it
Because you don't need no affirmative action
Affirm yourself and spring into action
Don't ever run from your potential
Because it'll chase you
And slap you in the face
Years later
In the form of regret.

-K

Public School Prodigy

Some of y'all only got the chance

to be one thing in life so far -
 you had interests turned majors turned fields of studies turned careers,
 But I got to be mad shit in one lifetime:
 I was a lunchtime table-beat maker, recording engineer if you will, grinding out rhythms for shorties to wild out to;
 I was a CEO of my own double-dutch game company, because when tick tock said the game was locked, you damn sure couldn't play;
 I was intel and liaison to an army of bad bitches, because someone had to instigate a fight, but not war on the front lines;
 I was defense attorney, judge, and jury in the courtroom of hallway arguments, myspace beef, and AIM drama;
 I was a professional chef - making a meal out of butter roll and 50 cent soda;
 A personal shopper when my friends wanted cheese fries to go with it;
 I was an artist when I doodled my name upon desks,
 and an interior decorator when I erased yours.
 I am a public school prodigy.
 The success of the state mandates.
 Keep your chartered schools, give me charter buses for field trips
 Keep your privatized education, give me private social workers.

Keep your straight and narrow one-track path to career life –
I want to be a jack of all trades.

-J

Was They Black?

I'm rooting for everybody black

Every Katherine Johnson
  Every Audre Lorde
  Every Michelle Obama in the making
  Every Shirley Chisholm
  Every Angela Davis
  Every Kimberle Crenshaw
  That said, I won't be attending the book-signing
  I'll be signing the book
  I won't sit in the lecture
  Because I'm the professor of it
  I won't just be voting
  Because I'm drafting the bills
  I won't be letting you
  Restrict
  Ignore
  Dismiss me
  I'll be the one you turn to
  For the solution.

-K

Black Privilege

I never realized

How rich I was
   Until I found out that some children's parents
   Never read to them at night.
   So when I called on them to read aloud in my classroom,
   They lost their voices because they had none to model after.

-J

Feeding Little Black Souls

I see in the eyes of young black children

A hunger, a desire
  To learn, to grow, to transform
  They see themselves in the brilliant black souls
  Preceding them
  I see that they want to believe
  The half-hearted words of encouragement
  From the mouths of people
  Waiting on a check
  I see them being reduced
  To what they can produce
  Instead of their untapped, unfostered talent
  I see future community leaders
  In the hearts of young black children
  Children, who in an age
  Where depression and anxiety
  Are finally being contextualized
  In black spaces, black academia
  Are already victims of these demons
  I did not face until high school
  Shine black girl shine
  Shine black boy shine
  For these are more than t-shirt slogans

They are rally cries for future generations
Born so self-aware that they are ready
To crack before age 12
I see their pain
But there's comfort in knowing
That their minds are the keys
To set themselves free of that pain
Black kids, shine.
Shine, shine, shine

-K

V

Here

Sometimes
You are just born a black girl
And not able to love yourself
Until you are a grown woman.

Jagged Edges

If I died tomorrow

I wouldn't wanna come back as nothing else 'cept Black.
   People always ask me why I say that –
   Ain't no other answer 'cept we just the shit!
   God could look me deep in my baby browns
   And promise me privilege
   And invincibility in the media
   Dominance over society
   Ability to do what the fuck
   Who the fuck
   And say what the fuck
   When the fuck I want,
   And I'd still reply –
   "Cool, I want it. Just make me Black."
   And God might be like, "Damn, well If I woulda known that,
   I woulda put more time in making your ass and not your stomach so
fat!"
   And he'd give me dap and send me back –
   As Black and fat as the day he created me!

-J

Twice as Hard, Half as Far

It's not enough to be good enough

I gotta be better than them
  Twice as smart
  Have twice the talent
  Put in twice the effort
  Be twice as resilient
  When they're shitting on me - got twice the attitude
  Get half the respect
  Two times as much restraint
  To not react to insults
  Always remember, don't take shit from no one
  But also remember to be
  TheFriendlyBlackGirl
  Carry yourself as the best there will be
  But stay humble - can't have them thinking you're stuck-up
  Break your back to be seen as less than equal
  Work against all that's systematic
  Growing up black you have to go over the moon
  And back
  And sometimes even that ain't enough

-K

My MacBook is Not a Notebook

There is something about the way a pen touches a paper

Something like a magnetic force draws the two together and creates an ionic bond that ignites
    Or maybe the bond is covalent - I could never get those things right.
    I like the way my pen calls my notebook's name
    Sometimes with a stark darkness that is undeniable and hungry
    Or maybe with a navy regality that demands attention.
    When my pen and notebook make love it makes me cry
    Their union excites me- I watch them impregnate my spirit with terms for toddlers and onomatopoeia for offspring.
    Cornucopias go clack!
    Tendrils go thump!
    Laptop keys are impersonal beings
    Their faces never unique under my inspiration
    My genius unmoving to them – Their expressions are forever QWERTY with rigidness
    The beauty of what they create irrelevant to them.
    Pens have personality
    Inquisitiveness in their ink
    And yet even still
    These keys keep me coming back.

-J

GOD.

I remember the first time I hated God

As a child,
   I shunned him from my life
   How dare he trap me in this black skin
   I wondered why I was
   The color of mud
   Why the first time anyone wanted to insult me
   I was "black" and ugly
   How could he love me
   How could he let my people suffer so
   Where was he when European ships
   Washed up on African shores
   When white hands brought lashes
   Down on black skin
   When we were raped
   And hosed
   And hung
   And shot
   I remember hating God
   And wondering where he was in my life

-K

A Letter to Instagram Memes

I hate going online and seeing posts like,

"Black girls' skin is made out honey, caramel, and magic."
    Nah fam, it's not.
    My skin is skin. Flesh and cells and shit.
    It's brown and sometimes black in the sun and gray when I wait too long to put baby oil on.
    Stop trying to make my blackness all edible.
    All ready for consumption.
    No favors are being done to increase my pride and self-esteem,
    It's just making me hungry and craving sugar I can't have.
    Stop trying to elevate me to super-humanness.
    I can't do it all.
    Black women can't save the world.
    I'm tryna save myself.
    Case and point, me looking at your honey-caramel comparisons got me wanting to eat a honey bun, and the devil is a lie.
    Some days, I don't feel amazing.
    I want to just go online and wallow in my not-amazingness and feel like crap for an hour or two.
    I don't feel confident, and don't want to be.
    Let me wallow in my anxiety and feelings of mediocrity!
    Ya'll accept it from Becky with the Good Hair every day!
    Let my skin be skin!

Let me be human!
Let me be normal!
Let me be!

-J

ThePrettiestLightskinGirl

She tells you you're pretty

She's real
  She's smart
  And as long as y'all have been friends
  You wanted to be her
  To you,
  She's cinnamon and cream's earthly creation
  She's caramel and honey's most beloved daughter
  And then there's him
  ThePrettiestLightskinBoy
  He's smooth, tall and plays basketball
  Walks like his middle name Adonis
  That likes the prettiest brown and yellow girls
  When he starts to fall for her
  You ain't surprised
  Only boy that likes you is your cat
  And he don't got a smile like
  ThePrettiestLightskinBoy's
  She's a woman
  Since age 10
  You ain't
  You still flat chested and black
  But she says you're woman enough

She don't let that word touch her lips
The word Lightskin
Like it's profane
Cuz she knows
That to an ugly black doll like you
Them pretty light skins be the devil
They end up with shallow boys
Who only like the prettiest brown and yellow girls
But still, she holds your hand
When you call yourself everything
But the child of God
She cries with you
Tells you you're pretty
ThePrettiestLightskinGirl
Tells you you're pretty
She's so ethereal,
that the word don't even sound like a word no more
The concept turns to gray
But you know she's real
And she's smart
And when you get home you sit
Inside your closet
Touch your face
See if it feels like hers
And finally, you like it
You wonder if ThePrettiestLightskinBoy
Would like it too

-K

Ch. 22

Because I was the CoochieSnorcher

I know that vaginas are true one eyed monsters.
   That they have power, do more than just coil in sight of penile objects
   Cry way less for men than our eyes do, and spend more time eating them whole with a
   lusty vengeance that in turn, makes men cry tears from their eyes and penile objects.
   I know that vaginas see and hear and think and know that they're a
   monstrosity that's just too fucking awesome for just being awesome to fuck.

-J

LOVE.

I remember the first time I truly loved God

He was not hiding from me
  I saw him holding out arms to cradle me
  And stroke my naps
  And remind my black ass that we all suffer
  But my skin is not a trap – it is a gift to be the color of the earth
  One to be envious of
  One to be emulated
  To be admired
  To be treasured
  He reminded me that my people are resilient
  And live lives of radiance
  And excellence
  Despite the pain he reminds me that none of it is in vain
  Kisses me on my forehead
  And tells me to be just as black and excellent
  As I am every single day.

-K

Acknowledgements

Thank you to my Mommy and Daddy! All that I am is because of you not only making sure that I put my education first, but that I pursued my other dreams as well. Thanks for helping Jaida and I become successful young women.

Thank you to my sister, for always being there for me and being my best friend from the moment I was born. I couldn't imagine my life without you as my inspiration and support system and I don't want to.

A HUGE thanks to my friends for all the moral support and for keeping me motivated and thank you to Nyesha and Sam for helping make this happen!

Thank you to everyone who has supported the "We Are Already Here" movement thus far. This is just the beginning.

-Love, Kendra

To my sister, K-dillz! You have always had my back since childhood, even when I didn't deserve it. This world doesn't deserve you. I love you! Thank you for creating this vision with me!

Thanks to my husband, Charles for the everlasting support. I love you!

Thanks Mommy, Dad, and Gloria for the constant encouragement. I love you! Thank you Nyesha and Samantha for your contributions!

Finally, thank you to my students for inspiration. You may not read this, but when I see ya'll, I see God.

In the words of Celie – "I may be black, I may be ugly, but dear God, I'm HERE!"

–Love, Jaida

Also by Jaida Renee and Kendra Ashanti

Visit wearealreadyhere.com for the e-book and upcoming releases!
Follow us on instagram: @wearealreadyhere

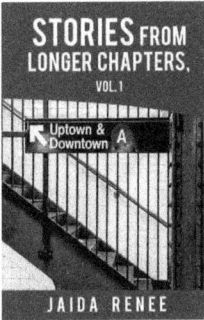

Stories from Longer Chapters

https://jaidarenee.com

From the heart of NYC comes this collection of vignettes about love, life, death, and identity through the eyes of young millennial urbanites. Get lost in the five boroughs amongst the characters as they navigate romantic relationships, familial ties, and higher education struggles. Stories from Longer Chapters, Vol. 1 is 5-story rollercoaster ride - one for each borough of our beautiful city.

This e-book is available on jaidarenee.com!

www.ingramcontent.com/pod-product-compliance
Lightning Source LLC
Chambersburg PA
CBHW031007090426
42737CB00008B/714